# The Motivation Manifesto

## *Unlock Your Drive and Achieve Your Goals*

# Table of Contents

# Chapter 1. Introduction

Unleash the untapped potential within you with "The Motivation Manifesto: Unlock Your Drive and Achieve Your Goals," our special report that energizes, enthuses, and empowers! This isn't your run-of-the-mill instruction manual; it's a beacon of light, a guiding force that ignites internal fires and fuels success-bound vessels. We've curated invaluable insights, practical wisdom, and effective methods to spur self-improvement, elevate ambition, and transform dreams into undeniable reality. Loaded with compelling narratives and action-oriented strategies, it's a definitive guide designed to pull you up from your comfort zone and thrust you into a realm of relentless progress and achievement. Buckle up, expect the extraordinary, and prepare for takeoff. This captivating report might just be the ticket you need to turbocharge your journey towards personal and professional success.

# Chapter 2. Unlocking Your Inner Drive

To unlock one's internal drive is to access the intangible engine within, propelling individuals towards the horizon of their aspirations. Moving beyond limiting beliefs, ego-driven fear, and self-doubt, this exploration opens the door to the untapped potential harbored within each individual.

## 2.1. The Source of Inner Drive

Often the most significant source of confusion or lack of action comes from a fundamental misunderstanding of the root of our inner drive. Individuals often believe this drive comes from external factors – promotion, wealth, or recognition. In reality, true inner drive comes by aligning daily actions and choices with deeply held values and goals.

Your drive could be guided by a desire for intellectual growth, a need for creativity, a longing for connection. Maybe it's philanthropy or simply the pursuit of excellence in any chosen field. By recognizing this, you can begin to cultivate your drive and use it to propel you forward. This comprehension of self is vital for sustaining consistent effort in challenging situations.

## 2.2. Cultivating the Drive

Understanding what truly motivates you is only half the battle. The real challenge lies in honing and maintaining your drive. It involves daily rituals, consistent reminders, and an unwavering commitment to your chosen path.

Start by creating a vision, grounded in your values. Define what success means to you, understanding that it might be radically different from societal norms. Paint a vivid picture and keep it at the forefront of your mind.

Next, establish specific, measurable, attainable, relevant, and time-bound (SMART) goals. These targets provide direction and allow you to measure progress. Having clearly defined goals helps maintain focus and provides motivation when faced with inevitable setbacks.

# 2.3. Fueling the Drive: Passion and Perseverance

Passion and perseverance form the very foundation of maintaining and enhancing your inner drive. Passion ignites your interest and fuels your performance, while perseverance provides the tenacity to withstand adversities and pursue your goals relentlessly.

Identify what you are genuinely passionate about. What energizes, excites, and motivates you? What interests or activities feel so intrinsically fulfilling that time appears to slip away? These passions form the heart of your drive. Coupled with an indomitable spirit to persist, they can create an unstoppable force.

# 2.4. Developing Adaptive Persistence

Persistence is not about blindingly pursuing an objective in the face of overwhelming obstacles or evidence contradicting your strategy. It's about adaptability – tweaking your approach based on feedback and changing circumstances.

A 'fixed mindset' sees challenges or failures as damning evidence of one's inability. However, an 'adaptive mindset' views these same obstacles as opportunities for learning, adjusting, and growing. To foster such a mindset, acknowledge failures, but don't dwell on them. Instead, extract the lesson and adjust your approach.

## 2.5. The Role of Resilience

Resilience is the ability to bounce back from adversity, disappointment, or failure, maintaining forward momentum, and constantly learning from your experiences. Your resilience, or 'bounce-backability,' is crucial in maintaining your drive.

Developing resilience involves embracing discomfort, fostering optimism, and taking decisive action. It requires appreciating that setbacks, hurdles, and failures are integral parts of the journey towards success. Use these challenges to learn, adapt, and grow stronger.

## 2.6. Accountability: The Missing Link

Holding yourself accountable is crucial in cultivating and sustaining your inner drive. Set yourself up for success by openly committing to your goals, enlisting support where necessary, and regularly reviewing your progress.

Accountability enables you to track your ongoing progress, offering an opportunity for celebration when goals are achieved. Recognizing your successes, no matter how small they might seem, further stokes the fire of your internal drive.

## 2.7. Summary

Unlocking your inner drive is a journey of self-discovery, self-mastery, endurance, and growth. Recognizing the source of your drive, cultivating it through vision and SMART goals, fueling it with passion and adapting your persistence, developing resilience, and holding yourself accountable are critical steps.

While this path is seldom easy, it is invariably rewarding – propelling you onto the path of lifelong growth, fulfillment, and achievement. Remain resolute and step boldly into the future, with your bolstered inner drive guiding the way.

# Chapter 3. Understanding Your True Potential

The journey to understanding our true potential begins with a simple, yet profound realization: each of us possesses an innate and immense capacity to achieve, impact, and grow beyond our current circumstances. We are not mere recipients of life's whims; instead, we are powerful creators shaping our destiny.

## 3.1. Preliminary Steps: Acknowledging and Accepting Potential

Underneath the rhythm of everyday life beats a heart of potential, available to each and every one of us. Every sunrise presents a new chance to inch closer towards our passion and purpose. However, one cannot unlock doors with keys they refuse to see. Hence, the first step to tap it is acknowledging and accepting its existence.

Humility fosters introspection—acknowledging both our strengths and weaknesses. One must also possess the courage to accept their potential unconditionally. This acceptance shouldn't be flavored with arrogance, but melted in maturity and magnanimity, understanding that with great potential comes great responsibility.

## 3.2. Introspection: The Mirror to Your Potential

To understand our true potential, we need introspection—an inward journey to discover our true selves. This voyage unravels dimensions of our persona, unvisited, perhaps even unknown. It brings into focus our attributes, skills, passions, and quirks that make us unique, highlighting the canvas on which we can draw our masterstroke.

Spend solitary moments away from distractions, engaging in mindful meditation and deep reflection. Ask yourself questions like, "What sets my heart ablaze?" "What do I profoundly enjoy?" "What are my strengths?" "Where lie my areas of improvement?" Such self-directed queries prompt detailed answers, shedding light on the contours of your potential.

# 3.3. The Role of Passions and Strengths

Our passions—those interests or pursuits that ignite our spirit—often harbor great potential. Leaning into them opens avenues of unprecedented satisfaction and success.

Moreover, our strengths—those inherent talents and trained skills we uniquely possess—signal another potential powerhouse. Leveraging them to solve problems, create solutions, or merely to express oneself, underlines our unique value proposition and shows us our capacity to effect meaningful change.

# 3.4. Embracing Challenges: A Path to Unveiling Potential

Staying within comfort zones rarely cultivates growth, but life's challenges—despite adversity and initial discomfort—often propel us towards untapped potential. Viewing challenges as opportunities instead of obstacles helps mitigate fear and apprehension, replacing them with a sense of adventure and thirst for achievement.

In facing these challenges, strive not for perfection, but progress. Each incremental step, each small victory matters. With each strife, we sharpen our skill, deepen our resilience, widen our perspective, and learn more about ourselves—voilà, another fragment of our potential revealed to us!

## 3.5. Growth Mindset: The Key to Unlocking Potential

A growth mindset—the belief that skills and intelligence can be developed—plays a crucial role in exploring and enhancing potential. A growth mindset embraces failure as a stepping stone to success, treating each stumble as a lesson, not an endpoint.

Adopting a growth mindset advocates resilience and persistence, casting aside the fear of failure. It enables us to take constructive feedback positively, learn from our experiences, trust in our capacity to improve, and confidently navigate the path to realizing our potential.

## 3.6. The Power of Purpose

Purpose—the profound reason why we do what we do—can be a driving force in realizing our potential. A clear sense of purpose provides motivation, direction, and a reason to persevere. Unearthing one's root motivations, values, and desires often illuminate our life's purpose.

Knowing your purpose can guide your efforts in congruence with your true potential, channeling your energy towards what truly resonates with your soul. This coherence between potential, purpose, and action sprouts a fulfilled life, bubbling with accomplishments.

## 3.7. Building the Roadmap

Post understanding the intrinsic aspects of your potential, create a roadmap towards achieving it. Dream big but start small. Break down larger goals into smaller, attainable ones, each acting as a stepping stone towards the ultimate goal. Remember, the journey to unlocking your true potential is a marathon, not a sprint.

# 3.8. Nurturing Your Potential

Understanding our potential doesn't mean it remains static; it is a dynamic entity that can be nurtured and expanded. Continue investing in self-improvement, acquiring new skills, gaining knowledge, and welcoming varied experiences in your pursuit of potential. Nourish your mind and soul with positivity and perseverance.

Understanding your potential signifies the beginning of an extraordinary journey – one filled with self-discovery, growth, and triumphant victories. Embrace it, explore it, and let it guide you to build an unforgettable saga of success and fulfillment.

While this journey comes laden with its share of struggles and setbacks, remember—they are but stepping stones, not stumbling blocks. Each effort, whether it results in success or failure, brings you one step closer to recognizing and unlocking your untapped potential. Painstaking patience, relentless resilience, unyielding strength, and firm faith in your journey are the keys to unleashing the formidable reservoir of potential that lies within you. Forge ahead, for the treasure trove of triumph awaits your arrival.

# Chapter 4. Mapping Your Journey to Success

Success isn't a destination, but rather a journey best navigated with a detailed roadmap in hand. To plot a course towards your goals, you'll need to answer some essential questions, embrace key principles, and follow a comprehensive strategy. The process involves understanding your starting point, defining your dream destination, and mapping your course.

# 4.1. Understanding Your Current Position

First and foremost, you need to establish where you are. It's paramount that you identify your current situation and evaluate your circumstances without reservation or self-deception. This frank assessment will serve as the foundation upon which you build your journey to success.

1. Assess your Skills: Evaluate your current set of skills and identify those that are truly assets versus those that need improvement. Reflecting on past experiences and past jobs can guide this evaluation. Discussing these skills with peers, mentors, or career counsellors can provide a fresh perspective to this assessment.

2. Analyze your Interests: Apart from skills, your interests significantly impact your motivation and job satisfaction. Ask yourself what activities you enjoy, what topics you could read about endlessly, and what kind of work makes you lose track of time.

3. Evaluate your Values: Your values influence your actions and decisions. They include integrity, freedom, creativity, social interaction, among many others. Identify your core values and

consider how they align with your current situation and future ambitions.

# 4.2. Defining Your Dream Destination

Equipped with the understanding of where you are, you can now start defining where you want to go. This goal, your dream destination, is a unique and personal vision that encapsulates your aspirations.

1. Setting SMART Goals: Ensure your goals are Specific, Measurable, Achievable, Realistic, and Time-bound (SMART). This technique ensures your goals are tangible and attainable, grounding your ambition in reality.

2. Visualize your Success: Envision what completion looks like. What will you be doing? Who will you be with? How will you feel? Visualization creates a vivid mental image of your desired outcome, making it easier to work towards.

3. Develop your Mission Statement: This encapsulates your goal and the path you plan to take in order to achieve it. A well-defined mission lays out the purpose of your journey, the objectives, and the behaviors and values that will guide you.

# 4.3. Plotting Your Course

After understanding your current position and defining your dream destination, next comes the task of mapping the route. This involves planning, strategizing, and deciding on the actions that will take you from where you are to where you want to be.

1. Identify Key Milestones: Break your journey into smaller, more manageable parts. Identify the key steps or milestones you need to achieve along the way.

2. Develop Action Strategies: Formulate strategies for every step of your journey. Outline what actions need to be taken, resources required, and potential obstacles that may arise.

3. Schedule Initiatives: Each actionable strategy needs a timeline for execution. Set a start and end date for each initiative and make sure they align with your overall timeline.

# 4.4. Keeping Your Course

The journey to success is inevitably fraught with challenges. Staying on course demands resilience, flexibility, and regular reflection and measurement.

1. Evaluating Progress: Regularly measure your progress towards each milestone and the overall goal. This will help you identify when you're off track and need to adjust your course.

2. Embracing Flexibility: Change is the single constant on every journey. As you move forward, there'll be unexpected events and unseen opportunities. Learn to adapt and highlight the ability to pivot as a key skill.

3. Building Resilience: Persistence in the face of adversity is a vital trait for success. Cultivate resilience to endure the inevitable bumps along the way while keeping your focus on the end goal.

Your journey to success is as unique as you are. By understanding your current position, defining your destination, plotting your course, and staying resilient, you solidify your path. Remember, the route to success isn't a straight line, but with a well-planned map in hand, you're prepared to overcome challenges and relish in the journey's triumphs.

# Chapter 5. Bringing Ambitions to Life

Understanding ambition is the starting point for any great undertaking. It is the powerhouse of your being, the driving force propelling you towards your goals and dreams. Without it, the path towards success can become convoluted, disjointed, and ultimately disappointing. Therefore, understanding and harnessing the power of your ambition is intrinsically tied to bringing those ambitions to life.

## 5.1. Illuminating Your Ambition

Never underestimate the importance of illuminating your ambition. Ineffectual as it might first seem, this act of genuine introspection will open doors to wider horizons than initially conceived. The thing about ambition is that it often resides within us, a hidden gem awaiting discovery. Take the time to sit in solitude, allowing your mind, heart, and soul to unravel the layers of your ambitions freely.

For illuminating your ambitions, start by questioning. What ignites your passion? What envisioning drives you to act relentlessly towards execution? The answers, though may take time, will reveal the deepest nucleus of your desire and purpose. This awareness will provide the momentum and direction to convert possibility into reality and potential into purpose.

## 5.2. Architecting the Blueprint

Every great creation stems from a detailed, exhaustive plan—your aspirations are no exception. Architecting the blueprint of your ambitions is the next crucial step. You're not just jotting down goals; instead, you are carefully constructing a roadmap that will lead you towards your ambitions. Write out the wide-ranging goals, intended impact, feasible action plans, and potential obstacles. Make these as detailed and distinct as possible for they are the bedrock of your ambition's manifestation.

The first component is the wide-ranging goals. These are the overarching objectives that embody the essence of your ambitions. From career progression to personal growth, ensure each goal is connected to your zeal and drive. Each goal should relate to an ambition, an aspiration you are inspired to achieve.

The second element is the intended impact. How will achieving these goals affect you and those around you? By understanding the potential impact of your ambitions, you can gauge their absolute importance and gravity. The greater the positive impact on others and yourself, the more compelling your drive to succeed becomes.

Thirdly, setting tangible, feasible action plans are integral for your ambition to move from the conceptual realm to reality. Infuse them with realism and periodic milestones to aid in monitoring progress.

Lastly, anticipate potential obstacles. Remember that challenges are not a sign of defeat, but opportunities for growth. Acknowledging them beforehand improves resilience, allowing you to adapt and overcome.

# 5.3. The Art of Goal Setting

Goal setting is a fine balance between finding feasible targets and stretching your limits. The power of setting SMART (Specific, Measurable, Achievable, Relevant, Time-bound) goals cannot be overemphasized. Take each of your wide-ranging goals and break them down into smaller, tangible objectives using the SMART framework. Doing so not only provides a clear trajectory towards your aspirations but also allows for progress tracking, constant motivation, and timely adjustments.

# 5.4. The Power of Consistent Action

Taking consistent action towards your ambitions is perhaps the most pivotal aspect of bringing them to life. Without consistent effort, even the best-crafted blueprint will count for naught. Consistency isn't about instant gratification, but a dedication to gradual progress. It's about showing up every single day, irrespective of the pace of progress, and pushing forward.

Create routines and habits that align with your ambitions. Make these actions an integral part of your daily life. The more you reiterate positivity, self-belief, and focused action, the closer you'll get to your ambitious goals.

To keep the momentum going, celebrate the small triumphs alongside the major ones. This practice nurtures the enthusiasm, motivation, and gratification necessary to stay committed in the long run.

# 5.5. Nurturing Resilience

Realize that the path to fulfilling your ambitions won't always be a direct one. Unexpected twists, disappointments, and roadblocks are part and parcel of any journey. Herein lies the power of resilience.

Maintain a growth mindset. See failures and setbacks as opportunities to learn and grow. When faced with obstacles, instead of giving in, change your perspective. Strategize, adapt, and find an alternative route towards your goals. This attitude, intertwined with determination, can turn challenges into stepping stones.

Your indomitable spirit coupled with an actionable plan is a formidable combination. This blend gives substance to ambition, transforms dream into purpose, and paves the way to achievement. As you traverse this path, remember to be patient, work consistently, celebrate progress, and foster resilience. Remember, your ambition reflects the heights of your potential - dare to reach for it, strive to attain it, and never cease to believe in its eventuality.

# Chapter 6. Overcoming Challenges: A Realistic Approach

It has been said that life is a series of challenges. Each day brings new obstacles to navigate, battles to fight, and problems to solve. But for each one of us, challenge embodies a different degree of complexity, a different level of struggle, a different path to eventual victory. In this journey of overcoming obstacles, we seek not only the right mindset, but also a tangible, realistic approach designed for practical application and tangible results.

Stumbling upon adversity, we often resonate with the age-old adage — 'the struggle is real.' But herein lies a question that demands our utmost scrutiny, 'How do we turn this real struggle into a real success?'

## 6.1. Embrace The Challenge

The first milestone in overcoming any challenge is acknowledging its existence and embracing it. Pretending that everything is in perfect order, or fleeing from the situation, won't make the obstacles disappear. Acceptance is an active and immediate release from the chains of denial. It grants us free passage to confront the situation, assess its gravity, and evaluate possible solutions.

Avoid the classic mistake of dwelling on statements like 'Why me?' Instead, change this narrative to 'Why not me?' The latter statement fosters courage and frames challenges as stepping stones enabling us to rise higher. Embrace challenges and acknowledge their roles as life's stringent teachers, imparting valuable lessons, molding our personalities and improving our resilience.

# 6.2. You Are Stronger Than You Think

Acknowledge that you possess the strength and ability to overcome these challenges. Despite the hurdles faced, self-doubt and feelings of incapacity often disrupt our willpower. We underestimate our potential and overvalue the weight of the challenge.

It's critical to foster a strong belief system, where self-doubt surrenders to self-belief, and fear succumbs to fortitude. Affirming that you are capable of managing the crisis, no matter its intensity, triggers your internal resources, empowering you to face the challenge head-on.

Remember that fortitude doesn't always roar. Sometimes, it's the quiet voice at the end of the day whispering, 'I will try again tomorrow.'

# 6.3. Develop a Solution Mindset

Once we've embraced the challenge and affirmed our strength to face it, the next step is to cultivate a solution mindset. Expend your mental energy on discovering solutions, rather than focusing solely on the problem.

Engage your logical brain to assess the situation objectively, identify the root cause of the problem, examine it from different angles, brainstorm, and generate a pool of possible solutions. Not all of these options will be effective, but the very process of considering alternatives encourages creativity and opens up new potential avenues.

# 6.4. Make a Plan And Act

With a pool of solutions at your disposal, it's time to forge an action plan. This involves choosing the most efficient solutions, compiling them into an organized timeline, and assigning yourself clear, achievable tasks.

A well-defined plan of action transforms vague intentions into concrete steps. It serves as a road map guiding you towards your end goal. But remember, plans without action remain lifeless blueprints. Now is the time to act, adjust, and evolve on the go.

# 6.5. Embrace Failure as a Learning Opportunity

In this journey of overcoming challenges, prepare to encounter bumps, detours, and red lights. There will be failures, but we must not allow these experiences to discourage us or derail our plan.

Remember, failure lends us an angle of insight that success often can't. It shines a light on our shortcomings and offers a chance to improve our efforts. It's an integral part of evolution – an opportunity to learn and enhance our effort and approach. In the grand scheme of our challenge-conquering journey, failures are disguised opportunities.

# 6.6. Practice Mindfulness and Patience

Amidst all these logical and action-oriented steps, do not neglect the importance of your emotional wellbeing. Practicing mindfulness, staying patient, and maintaining a positive frame of mind are pivotal.

Mindfulness tethers us to the present moment, making us more receptive to our changing circumstances. Patience follows suit as we learn to grow at our own pace, understanding that lasting change takes time, improvement is gradual, and the path to overcoming our challenges is rarely a straight line.

Our flight against challenges is a vast and complex maze. But remember, the labyrinth that once seemed bewildering and daunting slowly but surely yields its secrets as we navigate through it with perserverance, patience, and hope. Armed with this realistic approach to overcoming challenges, we learn not just to endure our struggles, but to transform them into foundations for our success and growth.

In this journey, you are your own guiding star, your source of light in the perpetual swirl of chaos. You own the leverage to define your path and rewrite your destiny. It's your narrative, your struggle. Make it your victory.

# Chapter 7. Nurturing Persistence and Funneling Focus

Persistence is not a trait we are born with, but rather, it is a skill earned through daily practice and discipline. There are undeniably countless instances in our lives when we have felt despaired and nearly succumbed to the siren call of giving up. Yet, it is in those moments resilience stands tall; it is in those pockets of life, we learn what it truly takes to develop unyielding persistence.

## 7.1. Grit: The Foundation of Persistence

Grit is not about how tough you are, but rather it is the indomitable spirit that refuses to quit, even in the face of overwhelming odds. The essence of grit lies in persistent effort towards a long-term goal, the unshaken belief that failure is just a stepping stone to success.

To cultivate grit, we must first identify our long-term aims - our so-called 'North Star'. Having a clear vision gives us the determination to push beyond our borders, to tirelessly chase after what we truly want, notwithstanding the hurdles and detours along the way. Then, breaking down the long term goals into manageable, actionable tasks helps make these aims more attainable, linking daily actions with our broader objectives.

## 7.2. Fun Is Not The Enemy

Popular belief often erroneously portrays persistence as a solemn, tedious pursuit. On the contrary, integrating fun into our journey towards goals can not only make the process enjoyable but also acts as a semi-permanent fuel for our drive. Finding and incorporating elements of fun in our fights keeps us motivated, lowers stress, and brings freshness and creativity to our approach. Some methods may include making your workspace more enjoyable, gamifying your tasks, or associating rewards with milestones to create positive reinforcement loops.

# 7.3. Resilience: Bouncing Back

There will be moments when the flame seems ready to die out, when obstacles feel insurmountable, and we must dig deep to find the strength to continue. Developing resilience at such times is paramount. Remember, failure is not final, but an opportunity to learn, grow, and then bounce back even stronger. Resilience can be fostered by maintaining a growth mindset, being adaptable to change, and by learning to manage stress effectively.

# 7.4. Unshakeable Focus

Focus is the lens with which we channel our energies most effectively towards reaching our goals. Yet mastering focus is perhaps just as challenging as nurturing persistence, with the constant influx of distractions that invade our daily lives. A more structured day, minimizing distractions, regular short breaks for mental refreshments, and dedicated time slots for deep work can help in fashioning a more concentrated mind.

# 7.5. The Confluence of Persistence and Focus

Combining the driving force of persistence with the pointed precision of focus, we can accomplish tasks quicker and more efficiently. This dynamic duo lays the foundation for stellar results; they turn dreams into reality and create pathways where none existed before.

# 7.6. Effective Time Management

Retaining focus and persistence over the long haul also requires efficient time management. Streamlining tasks, setting priorities, and using effective tools for managing work can go a long way in ensuring consistent progress on your goals while minimising stress and burnout tendencies.

Achieving extraordinary feats is not solely for the chosen few, the prodigies, or the special ones. It is within the capability of every individual, armed with persistence and focus. Once we internalize the essence of these qualities, we become the architects of our own success stories, turning the Impossible into I'm Possible. Through this journey of self-discovery and improvement, you will realize that success is not a destination; it's a lifelong journey of growing, learning, and becoming the best version of ourselves every single step of the way.

In conclusion, as you continue your relentless quest for personal and professional success, remember to arm yourself with the shields of persistence and the sword of focus. Your journey may be uphill, but the destination will undoubtedly be the pinnacle of what you could accomplish. After all, the view is always best from the top.

# Chapter 8. Empowering Mindset: The Catalyst of Change

Empowering yourself is an inside job. It begins within the confines of your own mind, among the very thought processes that weave the fabric of your perception and reality. You are not a passive player in a grim fate, but an active participant, a driver in life's grand voyage. Embrace this potential, foster it, and harness it.

First, let us explore the importance of mindset. Before we dive into the how, we should fully comprehend the why.

## 8.1. The Importance of a Positive Mindset

Every thought that dances across the stage of our mind sends ripples of consequence through our life. Positive thoughts can lead to immense joy, endless optimism, and even good health. Negative ones, sadly, can be equally as impactful in destructive ways. It's imperative that we learn to cultivate a mindset that invites and reinforces the positive, empowering aspects of our thoughts.

Think of your mindset as a garden. If a garden is left unattended, weeds can take over, crowding out the beautiful flowers and fruits. But with constant care and nurturing, your garden flourishes, sprouting vibrant blooms of empowerment.

# 8.2. The Components of an Empowering Mindset

A truly empowering mindset does not merely consist of relentless positivity or unyielding faith. It's a harmonious blend of various components, each critical and complementary to the others. Let's start breaking them down:

1. Confidence: A fundamental requirement to elicit change, confidence propels you towards conquering challenges and obstacles.

2. Creativity: Picture your journey as a constantly unfolding path. Creativity aids in finding new routes, sparking solutions, and challenging norms.

3. Resilience: Setbacks are inevitable, but resilience ensures they are mere bumps along your course, not dead ends.

4. Faith: It isn't just about religion or spiritual beliefs, but faith in your capabilities, in the journey, and in the outcome.

5. Adaptability: The world is in constant flux. The ability to adapt means you evolve alongside it, rather than being left behind.

# 8.3. Cultivating an Empowering Mindset

Creating an empowering mindset might seem like a Herculean task, but with commitment and patience, it becomes second nature. The following techniques can aid in fostering a change-inspiring mindset:

1. Be Mindful: Practice mindfulness to understand your thought patterns better. Recognizing them is the first step towards manipulation in your favor.

2. Affirmations: Integrate affirmations into your daily routine. They

can serve as powerful seedbeds for positive, empowering thoughts.

3. Embrace Challenges: Start viewing challenges as opportunities for growth, rather than struggles to be avoided.

# 8.4. Resilience: The Heart of an Empowering Mindset

Resilience often stands out among the essential components of an empowering mindset. It's the lifeblood that keeps you going, pushing you through the hard times to experience the peaks beyond. Becoming resilient requires time, but practicing the below principles can greatly expedite the process:

1. Acceptance: Life throws curveballs. Embrace the unexpected and accept situations as they are, not as you wish them to be.

2. Forgiveness: Let go of past regrets, guilt, and failures. Forgive yourself, and learn from these experiences instead of dwelling on them.

3. Gratitude: Cultivate an attitude of gratitude. Expressing thankfulness for even small victories can increase your resilience.

With the importance of positive thinking and resilience at heart, you're now ready to embrace an empowering mindset. It's not an overnight process; change takes time. But gradually, with each passing day, you'll notice a transformation within you. You'll become the catalyst for your change, a force of nature capable of surmounting any challenges that lies in your way.

Remember, you're the navigator of your life's voyage. Armed with the secret weapon of an empowering mindset, you are equipped to ride the tides of change and steer the wheel of your destiny towards your envisioned success. Let this power propel you forward, breaking the shackles of limitations, fostering unyielding resilience, and inspiring limitless aspirations. Keep propelling, keep soaring, and above all, keep empowering!

# Chapter 9. Adopting the Habit of Lifelong Learning

The sun of knowledge never sets; its rays permeate the darkest crevices of ignorance, shedding light and wisdom. By adopting the habit of lifelong learning, we pledge to keep our minds fertile, ready to cultivate new ideas, methodologies, and skills.

A journey of a thousand miles starts with a single step. In the same vein, the adoption of lifelong learning commences not with leaps, but with modest, continuous strides of inquisitiveness. A desire to know more, to understand better, to explore further is the cornerstone of this powerful habit. It's the fuel for the perpetual engine of intellectual and personal development.

## 9.1. The Pillars of Lifelong Learning

When one thinks of learning, oftentimes the image of a traditional classroom comes to mind. However, lifelong learning expands beyond the realm of formal education; it is far more comprehensive. It encapsulates self-learning, learning through experience, and learning from others. It is an unending journey that progresses with an open mind and an insatiable appetite for knowledge. Here's a closer look at its pivotal components:

1. Self-Learning: Picking up a book, listening to a podcast or indulging in an online course, the avenues of self-learning are aplenty. With the world at our fingertips, the scope for self-learning is boundless, and the only limitation that exists is the restriction we impose on ourselves.

2. Learning Through Experience: Experience is life's greatest teacher; it imparts lessons that are indelibly etched in the annals of our personal history. By embracing each situation — be it

pleasant or trying — as an opportunity to learn, we effectively turn each moment into an invaluable lesson.

3. Learning from Others: Everyone we meet, every interaction, harbors the potential to teach us something new. A constant exchange of thoughts, ideas, and experiences, meshed with active listening, enables us to learn from others.

# 9.2. The Benefits of Lifelong Learning

Embracing lifelong learning paves the way for an enriching life and myriad benefits that encompass personal development, career progression, and mental wellbeing. Let's delve deeper into these advantages:

1. Enhancing Cognitive Abilities: Lifelong learning challenges our brain, exercising it much like physical activity stimulates our body. This intellectual workout enhances cognitive abilities, improves memory, and arms us against cognitive decline.

2. Career Advancement: By staying updated with the latest industry trends, honing pertinent skills, and acquainting ourselves with emerging technologies, we enhance our competitiveness in the job market, fostering career growth.

3. Personal Fulfillment: Obtaining new knowledge, mastering a skill, or understanding a complex concept can be deeply rewarding. Lifelong learning nurtures a sense of accomplishment and enriches our lives with purposeful satisfaction.

# 9.3. Cultivating the Habit of Lifelong Learning

Establishing and fortifying the habit of lifelong learning can be a daunting task. But, like every habit worth its weight in gold, it requires time, dedication, and a handful of strategies honed to make the learning process enjoyable and sustainable:

1. Identify Your Interests: The process of learning is significantly more enjoyable when it is directed by personal interests. Identifying your learning passions can be the first step toward cultivating the habit of lifelong learning.

2. Set SMART Goals: SMART (Specific, Measurable, Achievable, Relevant, and Time-bound) goals give a clear direction to our learning endeavors. They keep us focused, help track progress, and promote a sense of achievement.

3. Leverage Technology: The digital era has simplified access to knowledge. Online platforms, educational apps, and webinars are game-changers, empowering us with a wealth of resources to learn from, wherever we are.

4. Embrace Challenges: Encountering obstacles is inevitable. Instead of being discouraged, view them as stepping-stones toward mastery. Remember, every mistake, every hurdle is a learning opportunity.

5. Practice Regularly: Consistency births proficiency. Regardless of learning what, regular practice reinforces knowledge, enhances skills, and embeds the habit of learning in our daily routine.

# 9.4. Nourishing the Habit of Lifelong Learning

Maintaining momentum in the journey of lifelong learning requires consistent nourishment, fresh perspectives, and the will to continue, even when the road gets hard. Here are a few ways to nourish the habit:

1. Build a Learning Network: Networks of like-minded individuals

bolster motivation, provide diversified viewpoints, and facilitate learning through shared experiences.

2. Dabble in Different Domains: Diversifying the learning horizon keeps monotony at bay. Venturing into different subject realms enhances versatility, ensures continuous mental stimulation, and broadens our comprehension scope.

3. Teach to Learn: The act of teaching not only solidifies what we've learned but also gives us the chance to look at it from different angles, promoting deeper understanding.

4. Review and Reflect: Regular introspection of what we've learned helps identify gaps in understanding, consolidates knowledge, and initiates queries propelling deeper learning.

Nelson Mandela once said, "Education is the most powerful weapon we can use to change the world." By embracing lifelong learning, we are not only transforming our world but also contributing to a broader global evolution. So, embark on this remarkable quest today. Ignite the flame of eternal knowledge, and let the sparks of wisdom illuminate the pathway of your successful and fulfilling life.

# Chapter 10. Rising from Failure, Racing towards Success

Modern society reveres success as the highest form of existence, the ultimate badge of honor, and the desired destination of every journey. Yet, it shuns failure, treating it like an unruly blemish on the clean, pristine surfaces of our lives. This perspective, however, is not only wrong but downright harmful. If we are to march steadfastly towards success, we must first understand failure and its invaluable role in our lives.

## 10.1. The Nature of Failure

Let us begin by understanding the dichotomy of success and failure. In any endeavor we undertake, we tend to categorize the outcome into two stark contrasts - success, the glorious triumph, or failure, the dreaded downfall. When we succeed, we celebrate, and when we fail, we despair. However, does failure truly deserve the despair it receives?

To change how we perceive failure, it is essential to explore its nature. We must comprehend that failure is not a dead-end, but a curve in the road. It does not signify a rampant, uncontrollable disaster; rather, it is an unexpected detour that presents an opportunity to learn and improve. Failure, hence, is not the antithesis of success but an integral part of it, a stepping stone leading to the lofty peaks of accomplishment.

## 10.2. Learning from Failure

Learning from failure is all about perspective - how we choose to perceive and respond to it. It might cause initial disappointment, anger, and frustration, but once the dust settles, we must strive to unearth the lessons hidden beneath the rubble.

Start by asking reflective questions like, "What led to the failure?" or "What could I have done differently?" Analyzing failure through such a constructive lens allows us to extract takeaways that could help avert similar mishaps in the future. Improve, adapt, and carry this new-found wisdom forward to your future endeavors.

Importantly, emphasize resilience. No matter how profound the failure feels, cultivate the courage to rise again. Winning is not about never falling, but about rising every time we do. Engrain this principle into your mindset, and embody its spirit.

# 10.3. Racing towards Success

The concept of racing towards success is metaphoric, as success isn't necessarily a race. Rather, it's a journey, a voyage of personal growth and improvement that progresses at its own pace. Chasing success begins with the audacity to dream, followed by the willingness to set robust goals, backed by meaningful action.

First, clarify what success means to you. It's unique to each of us—a distinct amalgamation of personal, professional, and emotional fulfillment. Success isn't solely acquiring wealth or power; it's a subjective construct that hinges on your values, ambitions, and happiness.

Second comes goal setting. Establish long-term goals to navigate your journey and short-term ones as milestones to help you track your progress. Make your goals S.M.A.R.T—Specific, Measurable, Achievable, Relevant, and Time-bound.

Finally, adopt a proactive, hands-on approach to realize your goals. Effort is the bridge between dreams and reality, so roll up your sleeves and get to work. Remember, steady and consistent effort fosters progress and edges you closer to success, one step at a time.

# 10.4. The Resilience Factor

Resilience is the backbone of transforming failure into success. It is when faced with adversity, resilience orients our inner compass towards ambition and teaches us not to surrender under pressure.

Nurture it by cultivating a growth mindset, remembering that skill and knowledge can always be enhanced with consistent effort and exploration. Embrace challenges as chances to evolve and see effort as the conduit to mastery.

Finally, reject the fear of failure. Never let the fear of striking out keep you from playing the game. Failure should be seen as a stepping stone, a platform for character building, and a chance to learn and grow.

# 10.5. Moving Forward

As we strive towards success, let's transform our definition of failure. Celebrate it as an integral part of the process rather than resenting it as the dreaded antagonist in your success story. Remember: behind most overnight success stories are years of invisible dedication, effort, and, yes, failure.

While we should learn from failure and resilience, don't forget to cultivate patience. As growth never occurs overnight, remember to revel in the journey rather than merely fixating on the destination.

By embodying this resilient, open-minded attitude towards failures and nurturing the right habits, we set ourselves on a trajectory towards success—a race not against each other but against our personal limitations, a race to manifest our dreams and ambitions, unapologetically and unceasingly.

So, rise from your failures, harness the lessons they provide, and brace yourself for a thrilling race towards success. Let's turn the narrative around failure and make it a powerful ally in our journey to success. After all, the key to winning the race isn't about never falling but about getting up each time we do.

# Chapter 11. Consistent Progress: Key to Lasting Achievement

The essence of achievement is not realized in a grandiose moment of triumph but found nestled within the consistent, incremental progress made every single day. Change isn't always immediate. Quite the contrary, lasting change - the kind that truly transforms a person, a project, or a pursuit - is usually a result of constant, measured progression. This chapter is dedicated to understanding this concept and unveiling the simple, yet robust, strategies designed to keep you moving forward, even when the journey gets tough.

## 11.1. The Mindset of Continuous Learning

We live in a world that celebrates sudden success, instant gratification, and quick fixes. However, to ensure unwavering commitment to your personal and professional goals, adopting a mindset of continual learning and growth is paramount. This involves tackling every challenge and viewing setbacks not as roadblocks, but as opportunities for knowledge acquisition and personal development. A steady pursuit of learning cultivates resilience, hones problem-solving skills, and progressively equips us with the tools needed to overcome challenges.

## 11.2. The Power of Daily Habits

Often, the difference between those who achieve their goals and those who fall short isn't talent, but the routine they follow. Cultivating daily habits, no matter how small, can play a pivotal role in achieving lasting success.

The power of daily habits lies in their capacity to create compounding effects over time. When consistent effort is exerted towards any endeavor, the gradual progress accumulated can translate into substantial gains.

For anyone serious about achieving their targets, creating a daily ritual committed to progress is non-negotiable. This could involve learning a new skill, enhancing an existing one, investing in personal development, connecting with mentors, or simply dedicating a set amount of time each day towards goal-related activities.

# 11.3. Overcoming Roadblocks

Trials are an inevitable part of any journey towards success. At times, you'll encounter obstacles that seem insurmountable, causing you to question your capabilities and even your goals. These moments, however discouraging they may seem, are an integral part of the process.

When faced with adversity, focus on your past accomplishments, however small or large, to summon the courage and determination to keep moving forward. Remember, every step you've taken has led you to this point, so don't let a single setback deter you.

# 11.4. Consistency: The Ultimate Advantage

The key takeaway from this chapter is consistency. Your dreams and ambitions are too valuable to be left to chance or sporadic effort. They demand frequent, sustained, and intentional action. The saying "slow and steady wins the race" holds true. By continuously applying effort, no matter how minor, you exponentially increase your chances of achieving your goals.

# 11.5. Putting It into Practice

The following strategies can help you maintain consistent progress towards your goals:

- **Set clear and measurable goals:** Know what success looks like for you and be specific about what it entails. Vague objectives dilute focus and breed unproductivity.

- **Schedule time for progress:** Make constant work towards your goals a priority by allocating specific time slots for them in your daily routine.

- **Track and evaluate your progress:** Document your daily achievements, however small, to provide a visible measure of your progress. This will help you stay motivated and focused on your journey.

- **Celebrate small victories:** Acknowledge and celebrate your progress, regardless of its size. This will boost your morale and create a positive feedback loop that motivates you to keep going.

By piecing together these elements, you craft a sustainable strategy for continued advancement towards your goals. The equation to success may vary from person to person, but the one constant that remains is consistent progress. It drives you forward, keeps you resilient during troublesome times, and ultimately guides you to your desired destination. This chapter's essence is to help you embrace this unwavering truth – that a commitment to constant progress is the key to lasting achievement. With consistent action, you'll find yourself accomplishing more than you ever believed possible. The journey towards achieving your dreams is not an event, but a process. As it unfolds, remember to stay open, stay resilient, and most importantly, stay consistent.

www.ingramcontent.com/pod-product-compliance
Lightning Source LLC
Chambersburg PA
CBHW072220290526
45794CB00007B/2818